Comments by Readers

A beautiful book. Deeply moving poems and essays by a young man struggling with adversity. He helps others by showing they are not alone.

Judith S. Rubenstein, MAT, Ed.D. (Harvard)
Publisher, Granite Hills Press™
Author of *The Christmas Present*

David writes of his world with courage and honesty. His story moves me, coveys how much suffering and love we are all capable of. These lines capture the essence of what he often wrote of, this holding of light and dark, which he seems to have experienced so very deeply:

I may be far from solitude
There may be no sign of peace
Somewhere in the ever widening universe
I will find release.

Marnie Cobbs
Poet and bookbinder
Eaton, New Hampshire

After suffering from a devastating stroke, through introspection and by the grace of God, the author of these eloquent poems and essays comes to a new self-awareness of happiness, peace, and love.

Alan Lippman, M.D.
Past President
Medical History Society of New Jersey

What a collection, particularly given the struggles David faced. Strong religious overtones, something frequently missing in persons facing emotional challenges. What I think is most important, at least to me, is his personal history. Thanks for sharing.

John A. Gergen, M.D.
Professor of Psychiatry, Emeritus
University of Southern Illinois

A Lesson in Reality is a moving and challenging reflection of David's life journey—all the more poignant in light of his significant disability and his forthright coping and recovery of his creativity and its ever widening and ultimately spiritual triumph along the path. His unvarnished honesty and introspection take the reader down the path of pain, loss and despair followed by a tortuous climb back up the mountain of meaning and self-worth through the grace of a God, whose many manifestations he explores and consolidates into a system that results in peaceful and encouraging arrival at a place where his spirit is full of light and fulfillment.

      I am reminded of a quote which he embodies in an inspiring and edifying manner:

" We are not human beings having a spiritual experience. We are spiritual beings having a human experience" -Teilhard de Chardin

Rev. Donald K. Hummel, D.Min., FAPA
Director of the Continuing Education and Formation
of Priests for the Archdiocese of Newark
Paramus, New Jersey

A LESSON IN REALITY

A LESSON IN REALITY

Poems and Essays

By
David Hedgcock Hill

Edited by George J. Hill, M.D.

HERITAGE BOOKS
2022

HERITAGE BOOKS

AN IMPRINT OF HERITAGE BOOKS, INC.

Books, CDs, and more—Worldwide

For our listing of thousands of titles see our website
at
www.HeritageBooks.com

Published 2022 by
HERITAGE BOOKS, INC.
Publishing Division
5810 Ruatan Street
Berwyn Heights, Md. 20740

Publication History
First edition: Hilltree Farm Press, 2004

Frontispiece photograph of David Hill by Eric Wagman Studio, So. Orange, N.J., 1984. The studio is now closed. Photograph of David at age 4 in 1959 by Cooper of Waltham, Mass., now closed. Back cover image of piano keys by Iguanat from Pixabay. Some of these poems were previously published in *Podium*, January 1991 and December 1999; and in *CPI Chronicle*, March 1997.

Cover designed by Debbie Riley

International Standard Book Number
Paperbound: 978-0-7884-2396-3

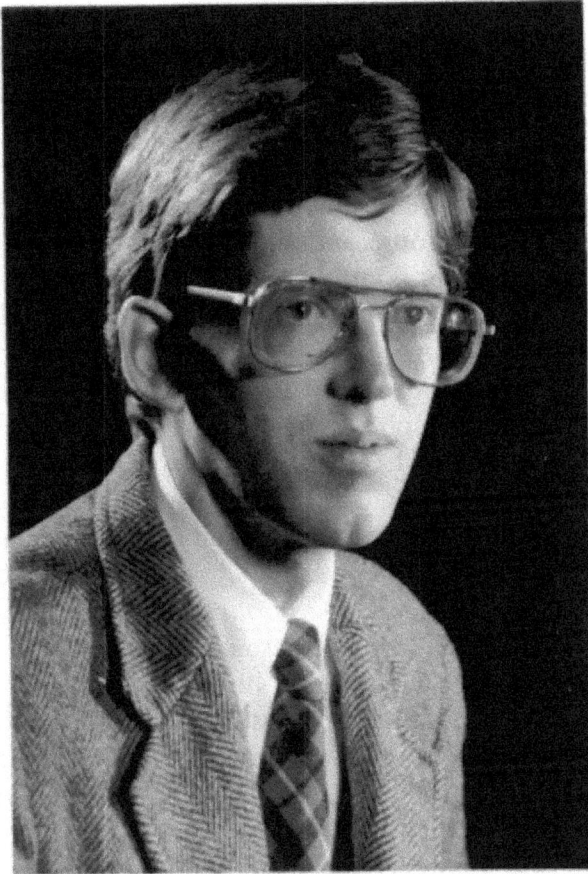

David Hedgcock Hill

Foreword

As long as I can remember, I've found inspiration in nature, contemplating my place in the scheme of things. As a little girl, I spent hours outside with the family dogs or exploring the woods behind my childhood home or in the fields that belonged to the neighboring farms. As a little girl, I didn't need proof of God's existence—I truly expected an angel around every corner—though that changed as I got older, a journey I chronicle in my book, *Everywhere Holy*. But through it all, I have come to know that people walk into our lives according to a divine plan.

I serendipitously met David's father, George, when he visited Grier School, an all-girls boarding school in the Allegheny Mountains of Pennsylvania, with David's granddaughter, Marcina. Immediately, I could tell George was a kindred spirit—a lover of words, nature, and someone very much interested in humanity. After spending much of the day together, I suggested that George and Marcina read Mary Oliver's collection of poetry, *Devotions*. I had no idea of David's poetry or that much of his words share similar themes to Oliver's own. I simply sensed George would like the collection and I was right: he did. Our chance meeting that day in July has unfolded into an unexpected friendship between us—two people who love language. When George shared this book, *A Lesson in Reality*, with me, I was honored.

Reading David's poetry is like peering into a soul, like inhaling deeply all the good and exhaling all of our own struggles, worries, and angst, despite the fact that maybe David struggled to do so himself. His words pay homage to the human struggle with understanding and believing that there is something bigger than we are. David's poems call us to question what it means to even be a human on this Earth— loving, losing, but staying on our path because of and even *despite of* it all. His words give us the opportunity to contemplate our existence, to be reassured of God's place in the *reality* of things—the tangible God who walks with us, shining his light in the darkness.

I welcome you into this collection of poetry, hoping that you, too, can spend time with David's eternal words, remembering that you are never alone. *A Lesson in Reality* is here to hold our hands as we continue on our journey of being human. What a gift.

Blessings,

Kara Lawler
Author of *Everywhere Holy* and *A Letter for Every Mother*
Director of Advancement and Marketing,
The Grier School
Tyrone, Pennsylvania

Greg L. Cooper, Waltham, Mass. - 1959

David Hedgcock Hill, aet. 4

Contents

Editor's Preface

David Hedgcock Hill was a poet, pianist, organist, and composer of music. Some of his works were published during his lifetime, but at the time of his death on January 4, 2004, at the age of 48, he left behind many unpublished items, both in manuscript and in his computer. His son-in-law, Jason Haught, recovered his computer files and scanned the items that were readily available at that time.

The title of David Hill's computer disc suggests that he intended to publish his collected poems under the title, *A Lesson in Reality.* I have therefore chosen this title for this collection of his poems and essays. The longest poem in this collection is "The Maker and the Poet." David Hill planned to set this poem to music in the form of a cantata.

Most of the poems in this collection were undated in the computer file, but they were probably written between 1991 and 1994. One was written in 1996, as a gift to his aunt, Barbara (Zimmermann) "Babs" Johnson. Another was written for his mother in 2000.

The poems and essays are divided into thematic sections for the convenience of the reader. They are generally presented within each section in the order that they were found in the poet's papers, although they were not arranged in chronological order. The untitled poems are identified by first lines, shown in brackets, viz.: [First Line of Poem].

George J. Hill, M.D.
Baltimore, Maryland
August 19, 2021

Author's Preface

Happy reading!
Though none of us has
absolute proof one way or
the other of God's existence
The journey to our own answer
often gives some treasured insights.
The one point of core importance is.
to respect each other's thoughts, desires,
and opinions, and respect the environment
we are such a strong part of because in
that realization we each become a little more
"Godly"   DHH — 1 September 1991

Author's Preface

Happy reading!
Though none of us has
absolute proof one way or
the other of God's existence
The journey to our own answer
often gives some treasured insights.
The one point of core importance is
to respect each other's thoughts, desires,
and opinions and respect the environment
we are such a strong part of because in
that realization we each become a little more
"Godly"   DHH 14 September 1991

The Maker and the Poet

THE MAKER AND THE POET
David Hill   August 1991

The Maker saw the sign
And knew his time had come
He put together galaxies
And soon he made the sun
He knew that when he'd finished
A new life had begun

The Poet then designed his words
In very special text
He realized that when he spoke
Others would be blest
He'd take the words that he had heard
And spin them into flax

The Maker told the Poet
As he looked into his eyes
You must take the words that you have heard
And draw up all the signs
That must have poured from other worlds
So sun would shine inside

The Poet asked the Maker
If his work would soon be done
He waited for an answer
To fall out of the sun
"His task would never be complete
Until death he'd overrun"

"THE POET'S CALLING"

The Master spoke his presage
And the Poet had no fear
As deep inside the homage
He must pay had been made clear

He could not lose sincerity
Of doubt there was no trace
He must put an end to
All failing earthly ways

"THE CURSER'S VOICE"

In his journey to perfection
As he traveled to the light
The Poet found his fate
Had slowly faded out of sight

He turned another rune he heard
One different than before
As if coming from another world
It choked him to the core

As he looked in silence
He struggled for a choice
The root of all violence
Was in the Curser's voice

He had to quench his anger
He had to thwart all good
The Curser looked for danger
As amazed the Poet stood

At once he felt confusion
For once he heard his call
He prayed the Curser's delusion
Would not cause his fall

"THE CURSER'S LOSS"

As he stood in wonder
A voice came from above
He hoped the voice of torture
Would fall to the way of love

He knew in blindness, once he stood
This hate could not go on
He called in meekness, knowing good
There the Maker would live on

Amidst all that he had heard
A plaintive call rang out
It sang, the Maker as a bird
Freed all his pains of doubt

Again, the Poet strengthened
Since he knew his time had come
The voice that he had listened to
Would lead him to the sun

"THE VICTORY"

He stumbled and he faltered
As down many roads he ran
His faith it never altered
As he filled the Maker's plan

He knew the roads were twisted
As he ran to meet his end
In place of hurt enlisted
He'd always found a friend

At first, he felt his fall would come
As on the trail of doubt he'd run
Oft blinded by an evil sun
He smiled, a new world had begun

There the Maker saw the Poet
Tears streaming from his eyes
"You took the gold as it had flowed
And spun it into flax"

A thread when wrapped around the soul
Brought good where it was lacked

Spirituality,

Friendship, and Love

Spirituality, Friendship, and Love

[I cannot Cry in Anger]

I cannot cry in anger
Because there are others who do not seem to hear
When I try my hardest to soothe my fear
I see no more than emptiness
When I look inside myself
I want to run away
To something that will let me be
What I never could have been

[You Have Given Me Such a Gift, God]

You have given me such a gift, God
This patience inside of me
Because You know how long I will live
What You will do with me
Is forever changing
And will grow inside my heart and mind
As long as I know
Your love will keep me strong

Light Passage

It is a light of peace
Giving me assurance
As my courage fades away

I am graced with this newfound strength
I am holding on to new tomorrows
I am comforted by wise yesterdays

I am content
As my fear melts away
Into a nether world eons beyond

A voice within me has answered
A song within me has been sung
A verse within me has spring forth
My soul has welcomed the awakening

Boon Light

The moon soothes my soul
As I pass under its light
I am refreshed
I am freer than I once was

Now that my heart has
Welcomed this joyous vision
I will remember this night
For all its beauty

It has awakened in me
Something I had feared
Was long gone
Fallen into emptiness

I am not alone
I will choose
Between the entanglement of the past
And the reverie of the present

For I feel the presence
Of a spirit greater than mine
My mind has welcomed the freedom
Strength has entered me

It has given me the courage
My heart has welcomed the solace
To move on
I recall my past

Times when the moon
Was as bright as it is now
Those times are fresh
Within my mind

31 October 1993

The Challenge

Don't tell me of the laurels
You think you've won so easily
Just tell me of the heartaches
You've met within your agony

I want to pass through the gate
That holds in all the cruelty
But I know I'll want to wait
Until I know you've been there too

I know that we can share forever
Whatever we can find together
Searching through the mazes that we've run
Through the snowdrifts under the winter sun

We must share all the anger
We must share all the fear
We must share what's deep inside us
To find what's brought us here

So tell me of the pathways
You're walking every day
The windings and the turnings
Will help us find our way

To Seasons Hence

I walked across the frozen snow
As oft before I quick had done
 Once looking up into the sun
I'd then race to the peace I'd know

I wondered if I'd find the glow
Upon this ground that I had run
Looking out at a life undone
Cold from the wind which through me blows

I'm awed as now I think of days
Within which rest could not be found

But I'll look now for a sun to rise
Where I'm soothed so by her rays
So, other globes above the ground
And other sod beneath my eyes

Stone Age

I walk through a petrified forest
The trees are so frozen and bare
They have fallen through tortuous tempest
They rot, for there is no life there

Though the roots are tough as emerald
So tempered, hardened and strong
Each branch needs to be sated
With breath to move it along

They have rested for aeons
And not once were they touched
By the life-giving freedom
They have longed for so much

I stand at the edge of this oft traveled path
Whose solitude fills me with awe
I yearn, for this journey my yet be my last
To watch as these trees reach their thaw

Friends

Along the widening abyss of life
Where day blends tenderly with night
The joyful hours will never end
As long as we are with a friend

The sun will set as daytime wanes
We have soothed out aches and pains
And wait in home for coming sun
A chance to bind our souls as one

Years will pass and time will change
The struggles will have rearranged
The times within our hearts and minds
Where solutions were hard to find

We won't regret the times we've spent
We won't forget the peace we've met
We'll hold on to the very end
Now we've learned to live as friends

The Statue and the Strands

When we brush away the tarnish
That's scattered through our lives
What's left inside will tell us
That indeed we will survive

We now rebuild in honesty
The walls that were torn down
As we paint upon our tapestry
The feelings that we've found

Each voice we hear reminds us
That the substance in our heart
Is only there to bind us
To the fire beyond the sparks

In the end the sculpture stands
Fettered not in pain
But opened to the sea-strands
That longed to free again

Ode to a Grecian Urn: Part II

You have seen the urn burst into shattered fragments
Amidst the present
Those shards of the past have fallen away and collected in a heap in
      the corner
They are now buried in the dust ... useless

Do not sweep them up for there are still a few small pieces
Which can be brushed off and united into a cogent form
The jumbled vestiges of past separation seem to call out
To be joined together in harmony
Tied in unison, from a point where they were once lost
And now renewed

The form is visible now as it displays its subtle beauty – a   relationship
There are indeed scratches, mars and other flaws
But it was not meant to be perfect, only real
Only a reflection of that which we cherish the most ourselves

Rights of Passage

The truth is often hard to face
But you can accept it slowly
Take a little time for ease
And don't get in a hurry

What is revealed to you
Will carry you from old to new
From dark to light
From foolish to wise

Unity

As long as I am on this earth
I have no need to fear
For there is beauty and kindness
To be found all around me
And my Lord and Savior
Who watches me as I travel here
Will not let the lightning strike me
Or the thunder threaten me with its roar
I will look up to the skies in awe
And pray that God will give me more
Of this all-encompassing euphony
This ever-moving band of light
That awakens me when I slumber and
Sings to me in the night

Awakening

Once the chancellor of solitude had uttered
That peace must be present for all to see and share
The Minister of Music could be seen by all who were aware
That change must soon take place in a way that satisfied
All those who from the din had hidden and in agony cried
His message would be much the same
A presence of loving harmony where all could hope to gain

A peacefulness of mind and a gentle solitude
A freedom from that which brought them aches and worry
Their lives would be joined together again
And there would be no need to hurry though the craft
That called them each and every day

To a vitality of mind and a knowledge that there was
Sustenance waiting quietly for them
When they returned to their brood
At this moment of growing peace
Their fates had all been sealed
A new mission waited for them and a purpose was revealed

Published in *CPI Chronicle* 1 (no. 5, March 1997), 3

[Happy Birthday, Aunt Babs]

There is a certain rhythm that beats through our lives
A fortitude of knowledge that keeps us strong in our joy
Until and after our years number fourteen times five

Each passage of each year has new treasures waiting for us
Which will we hope convince us
To do what we know is the best
As surely as we did when we danced through our youth

The songs still play within us
And the sun is just as bright
As we begin to see
Our lives are perpetual day
With no indication of night

Happy Birthday, my dear Aunt Babs
May this eightieth decade you see before you
Be a never-ending chance to see beauty in all that you have

22 July 1996

R.I.P.

The knowledge that you gain from time
Will help you sit with peaceful mind
With positive and pleasant air
The freedom to believe and care

When the final days have come to pass
Your body lives, beneath the grass
All you've hid within your soul
Finally, will keep you whole

Sometimes

Sometimes I cannot find
The lines of poetry that will express
What I feel inside
Are they lost?
Am I lost?

Will they come to me when I am sad?
Will their gentle rhyme make me glad?
To be sure, I do not really know

I only know that God is the one who makes them pure
He may have found a way to keep them safe
Until he gives them life and gives them to me

[I May be Far from Solitude]

I may be far from solitude
There may be no sign of peace
Somewhere in the ever widening universe
I will find release

Life's losses are not forever
They simply widen my vision of you, God
For You are the brightest light in the sky
You are the fulfillment of every dream

Dearest God, you have brought light to me in darkness
Opened my eyes so that I could see
In the deepest part of me
The love You are because You are real

Passion Play

The passion that commences
Now that you've found yourself
Is one which shared among us
Can bring an inner wealth

It matters not what tool you use
To mold your inner realm
But merging with another's views
You can produce a calm

Each shade of anger, hurt and pain
You draw from deep within
Brings a heightened knowledge of
The freedom that begins

A start of something treasured
A victory for battles fought
Your passion is unmeasured
Since it flows straight from your heart

The rivers that it melds with
Keep flowing to a sea
That sashes out the harshness
Replacing it with peace

The waters of our passion
Must never cease to flow
Since therein lies the freedom
That we must make our goal

[In these Silent Motionless Moments]

In these silent motionless moments
I am not in any way alone
When by myself I sit
A deeper more peaceful part of me
Has found itself a home
And will dwell deep within me

In every moment I am alone
The peaceful Tao within always lets me see
That I am a part of everything around me
And will forever be free
As long as I am aware that
I am a part of everything around me

Al(one)

What separates us
From this great transmorphic world
We exist in moment to moment
Year to year

Is there some act
That must be performed
Visible to all around us
But perhaps unseen by ourselves

Is there some message
Which must fly rampant from our being
However apart from
The outside seeing

No, there is nothing
Which awakens ourselves
Outside our own knowledge
Of who we are in our solitude … and its reality

Past Recaptured

Where was the voice, unheard
That made finding you so hard
What riches lost in youth
Hid so deeply in all your truth

Was something lost inside your mind
A piece of love you could not find
A broken fragment of your past
Or reason that you hoped would last

When first you looked at frightened young
To place the words upon your tongue
Did you then in haste begin
To bring them along, lost hope within

As oft as you have looked back now
At times when you have wondered how
Your rhythm broke away from you
To find it now, you must be true

[You Must Move On]

You must move on
You can't stand still
And hope to climb the hill

You said look up
You'll reach the moon
If you don't look down too soon

You must grow strong
You can't be weak
And find the goal you seek

You must follow close
If you hold fast
You'll soon be wise

But only if you listen hard
And persevere in all you do
Yes, hold on fast

Your heart will lead you through

[When the Sun Shines Upon Me]

When the sun shines upon me
I waken and begin to see
Everything inside me has good to share
The warmth it brings is a light pointing the way

To the wholeness that lives inside of me
That makes me fully what I am
Once a youngster filled
With love for all around him

In that Love was a Greater Love that touched me
And enlightened me
Slowly as I began to grow
Wondrously I was reborn

I began to see that the Buddha
Was always waiting patiently within me
To bring from me the best Love
I could ever know

June 29, 2000

Light Touch

Light Touch

Ifdom

There is no peace in Ifdom
I or the miscreants cannot cheer
They say that if you do not yell at me
You may have some silence here

You cannot have the peace of mind
That you so deeply need
Because I do not care at all
About you

Because you will not let me blast
The music you call noise
Around you in the morning
When you are seeking joy

Spring

In roasting Spring weather
The kind-hearted ice cream man waits as David
Chooses a drink to cool off in the toasty Spring evening
As overly playful children bounce around him screaming
      wildly
As they push each other out of the way to get frozen treats
And David goes home

What Happened the Week Before You Were Born?

Goodbye
There's something in my head and it won't stop buzzing
Somebody hit a mallard down on Fulton Street
Why not buy some new shoes Friday
For Aunt William's 14th week anniversary?
Should we sit on the pink bench or the blue one?

Later on
I just ate the biggest skyscraper ever wrote
Why don't my feet stop singing?
There's a corn in my ear and I
Can't get enough of it
How about going down to the airport for a swim?

Hello
I'll see you yesterday
Whether it matters or not
So what
My teeth just fell out
And I have no idea how to put them back in
Perhaps my herpetologist can stretch my fingernails
I really miss being in the next century
Let's order take-out Ethiopian Goulash

I don't know
The slate next to the fire hydrant cracked again
Maybe Gorbachev will free the slaves next week
Wanna swim across the Gobi Dessert?
2 cups salami
4 figs
A dash of tomato juice
13 soft boiled eggs
1 cantaloupe
    Stir until nothing happens
    Bake at -36^0 until underdone
    Chill
    Then throw out

Now, wasn't that the worst Frank Sonata you've ever touched?

Back at the ball game
The score is 15-hate
With the referees loaded (3 outings to go)
I've had about all I've gotten used to
Except for Grandma and she's born again
What does the newspaper say about my lithoscope?
Let's write "Dear John Paul" for a toothpick
Hello, what's that?
You have a tennis ball stuck in your abdomen?
We'll have to perform a radical Capriati!

A pastry with a hole in the middle big enough to put your arm
          through
What is a Bundt?
I do not believe in reality
Therefore I don't think
THEREFORE I AM NOT!

Good morning!

Open Passages

As each textbook opens, I am
transformed into something between a
scholar and a blithering idiot

As each chapter speaks, I constantly
balance what I know with what I do not –
hoping to move upward in the process

As each page turns, I calculate the worth
of the effort I expend trying desperately
to look toward the future and not become

LOST

21 January 1994

Anger and Despair

Anger and Despair

Silence

She listened but did not hear
As choking, the words crawled from my mouth
I only wanted what she could not deliver
The satisfaction of knowing who I was

She had little knowledge of my inner presence
For she built a wall too high for me to break down
I would be happy simply to climb it
So I could look deep into her thoughts

She lay inside a fortress
Made of cold, hard granite so tight
I would not be able to open its doors
For pain has locked me out

I wish to gain entrance to this ivory tower
I cry for I have been locked out for so long
I call for future generations
Who with their challenge hope to grow strong

The Restructuring

Thus the priest of solitude
Would come one busy day
And bring peace to all of Ifdom
So all its boarders could in unison play

They longed to be together
With those they loved the most
All they wanted was some quiet
So they would have some hope

The artists kept on creating
As they had done so oft before
They wanted something to hold on to
That they knew could make them sure

That they could live in tranquility
Totally free from pain
And the rising storm around them
That continually bored into their brains

Hunchback:

The Hunchback Inside of Me

I am Quasimodo
Ringer of the bell
My only purpose in this life
Is to ring the hourly church bell so others may be
     pleased
Most will look at me as the animal that I am
But there are just a few who will see me as good
And let me descend from my invincible tower
And let me see them for what they are
Precious jewels which shine in my eyes and brighten
     up my life
And I will polish them with my hands and with my
     soul
And they will smile at me knowing that they are whole
They are part of me and I am part of them
All I crave is to feel my heartbeat once again

[The Beast that Has Ravaged Your Soul]

The beast that has ravaged your soul
Has left from you; now you are whole
The meat he has taken from your heart replaced
When you made a new start

Days fly faster now
That life has become new
Full his grace will flow
For he is blessing you

The seraph now holding your hand
Will walk with you to promised land
Teaching you a message clear
That you should heed as well as hear

The loaves are leavened
And endless wine is poured
Be faithful as you near
The golden glory of the Lord

There are many of us here who are struggling with loneliness. We have tried to tell ourselves that there are none who feel the way we feel. However, all it takes to break down our walls is a simple "hi" as we walk down the corridors here, or a few moments during the day just to reach out. Remember, if you reach out, you will get back a little more than you expect.

So let's make this a year of friendship for each other.

Published in *Podium* (January 1991), 5

As a Child Lost

I am the beast of terror grown
Who in the midst of night, past dawn
Upon the passing edge of eve
Did upon a youth relieve

Hard bent passions of ages past
Terror that had held me fast
An answer I had only sought
To why my precious time was bought

By one much older then than I
Who had no tear within his eye
But anger deep within his pate
Pursuing me in hateful pace

Did he wish me endless harm
Or just to hold me in his arm?

The Swell

I stand amid the growing screams
Which cannot be silenced
Because they are of drowning hearts
That deeply long to feel

They are filled with profanity
Which mills from the lips
Like oily waves along
A shore of garbage choking!

They are chased back and forth
Through the dormitory like
A thousand hamsters on their wheels
But going nowhere

Their terminus seems lost in nothingness
Inside a cave with unending
Depth and darkness
But there's no escaping its presence

15 May 1992

Metal Memories

You scramble through your solitaire
On a weekday afternoon
And wonder if the thoughts you share
Will help you through your gloom
Will they ever matter
All those metal memories?

You shudder through your slumber
On that weekday afternoon
And hope that in your kaleidoscope dreams
You will awake quite soon
Will you ever breathe
In those metal memories?

You look around at faces
In the glow of afternoon
You sense they are familiar
As they've far too often been
Will they fade into subconsciousness
And never rise again
Somehow … metal memories

You listen to the screams
In that fading afternoon
And hope that in the sadness
They somehow know you care
Yes, you will awake quite soon
From your metal memories!

5 May 1992

Under the Shadows

The feeling of silence
Locked in a tomb
Of fast-moving illness
Which heightens your gloom
Your body is stricken
By a virus of death

Eating away at your soul
Until nothing is left
Your appetite lessens
And your body grows weak
Your only nutrition
Is the words which you speak

You are caught in the midst of
The fire that is AIDS
You are trembling with doubt
As you struggle to save
All the peace that has left you
In those moments of hate

Your words become stuttered
As they crawl from your throat
When your passion is uttered
It is still as a ghost
Your death is a vision
Far off in the minds

Of those who have failed
In the torture you find
You pray that your silence
Will cease to exist
You yearn for the guidance
That love can unleash

Mideast Madness

Saddam took the rules
To change them to fit his plan
He tried to make us fools
But fast on our ground we stand

He bruised tikes
Men, animals of the earth
He broke the hearts of families
With his sickened childlike mirth

We will overthrow the demon
Who tries to destroy our world
We will turn his wrath against him
As our flag becomes unfurled

He killed his own armed forces
In a rage to meet his end
He assaulted all humanity
But still we must defend

In all his vile insanity
He never gave a thought
Of peace for our earthly family
In his mad, barbaric plot

We will overthrow the demon
Who tries to destroy our world
We will turn his wrath against him
As our flag becomes unfurled

The Environment

and

Native Americans

The Environment and Native Americans

Larval: Then Life

She spread my wings when I wasn't looking
Touching a part of me that had been silent
Suddenly it has found life!

I was no longer in my cocoon
Shedding hers has given breath to us both
Hopefully we gained our sight

We flew across the same sky
Entwining our wings for a moment
Watchfully we looked on the wideness of our worlds

Rain

The rain creates a symphony
Of ever drifting beats
That touch the deepest chambers of my heart
In a rhythm all their own

Then the raindrops fall again
They collect the air around them in
A constantly closing net
As they echo all around me

The pitter patter of little beats
Wakes me from my sleepy dreamland of nonreality
And the raindrops fall again
I have been touched by a powerful but gentle peace

Ode to an October Morning

One morning I arose
The smells of cooking filled my nose
With pensive solitude I'd slept
First I awoke and then I wept

For rattling sounds around me roared
Ones that now I cannot ignore
I wondered then how day would pass
Was my agony now so crass

That passing moments had no use
In a day not filled with ruse
I must however now assume
As I sit now within my room

That this day will preclude all rest
From becoming fully manifest

To the Wild

Upon the mantle of this day
I look out into the sky
And feel my senses heightened by
A placid freedom on its way

A skein of soaring geese, their fray
Built across a radiant sky
A field of armoured hawks does fly
Above me on as ground I lay

I feel so small amid the bliss
Around me on this glowing globe

Now the knowledge in me grows
As each man around me knows
That future worlds must have the hope
Of seeing what we soon will miss

Hope for a Dying Globe

Why have you now forsaken this ground?
The sky has turned an acrid green
From smokestacks pumping endless filth
The rivers flow with choking garbage

Lives are lost

Man has simply sought freedom from daily toil
Simplicity in packaging has caused the spoil
Of miles of land, we once enjoyed
Flushed now into our seas, so cruel
The refuge which could be our fuel

Beauty falls from view

Look now upon this damage done
Feel the purging heat of sun
Burning through our atmosphere
Where once the air to breathe was clear
Greenhouse gas has scorched the clouds
And left us 'neath a smothering shroud
Can we endure this heartless pain?
We must give earth her life again!

Cry of the Man-Ape

Oh, man
Do you know where you're going
You've wandered across the sands
Past the trees from barren lands
How time has been cruel to you
As you wonder where you stand

Through many years you've trod the ground
Painful cries at every sound
The songs of pounding tribal drums
Beat through your soul as close they come
And isolation pulls you down

You walk amid the blood ruins
Of your tortured wife and children
Wondering why you've lost them now
Can you bring them back somehow
Or has your lineage reached its end

CRY, YOU SADDENED SOUL

The tears you weep now make you whole
Bring back the joy you lost your past you love
With the fruit of tribal bands
Let your life begin again!

14 September 1991

Progress?

Step up that hill
Where once you ran
As a child

Walk down the banks
Of that river where you
Used to float paper sailboats
      In your youth

Skip along that road
Where you used to share
Memories with endless
    friends
From bygone days

Walk up to the porch
Of that cozy little house
Which held you so close and
    secure
When you were so young

BUT WAIT!

That hill is now garbage
A heavenly mound
Changed to a tower of filth
By countless careless big spenders

That river has hardened
By the heartless tossing
Of detergent, excrement, and rubbish
The list goes on and on. It is so sad

The road is now a freeway
Driving everyday hominids to the middle of their hustle and
    bustle
To find more riches
To destroy more land

Take one last look at that porch
Before you mature
It is not quite the same since the rich and shameless
Turned it into a shopping mall

As you look past the ages and see
What has been lost
Remember the land that once brought us such joy in youth
Can only be replaced by returning that joy to its mother soil!

[Oh, Ben of a Thousand Voices]

Oh, Ben of a thousand voices
You with many tongues
In a host of different rhythms
Your song since you were young

Those voices for a chorus
With souls from lands far away
The winds and waters hush
When the Heavens hear you say

Let me sing to your soul in sadness
Let me call to your heart in joy
Your voice in all its wonder
Will soothe me when I cry

A light from a thousand moonbeams
Glows whenever you speak
It awakens in your dreams
To free the ones who seek

Your tongue has many branches
To answer many calls
You speak, your spirit dances
At your feet your burdens fall

Oh, Ben of a thousand voices
You speak with dancing tongues
To all the different faces
You knew when you were young

You've walked across the plains
From age to age and then
You listened to the pain
That the Great Spirit came to send

In a blinking of a vision
You saw a shining light
One that glowed above the world
As it shone throughout the night

You know you've seen the spirits
So many times, before
They would shower you with strength
As they did in days of yore

As your earthly strength was a complement in kind
To all the trials that you've been through
And all the tears you've cried
Always brought your vision back to you

You have wrestled with the past
And tried to rebuild again
A world that would last
Through the sea of pain

You saw another vision
More peaceful than before
That told you that you would win
Back your ground from the White Man's war

Your Spirit grew and soared above the ground
Shining through the faces of all who shared the land
Yes, in the future the old ways will be found
And we will once more share the earth on which we stand

Wisdom From Beyond

I have walked across the plains of a past life
And remember those who touched my heart
I dream dreams of keeping myself alive
As I nourish others through the Great Spirit's words

I have held the creatures of his bounteous caring
And listened to them sing to me at night
I have raised my voice to Him as He soothed my longing
And told the land that our spirits are one

I have tightened my grip on the past life
Knowing that I cannot let it go
It has brought strength amid my roaring cries
And warmed me as the Great Inca's glow

I have called for my worldly family to join me
And I did not care about the color of their skin
I only wished them to learn as I and those before me
Knew the Great Spirit has made us kin

Now I look around at all the wisdom He has left me
And feel there is no limit to its great worth
I call out that others might share what I have seen
I sing for ours is truly a united Birth

Published in *Podium* (December 1999), 31

Fading Beauty

Transcutaneous road
Cut across our lands
Like a spear through the bison's heart

The Caucasian said
He would lead us to opportunity
And help us survive

WE ARE CHOKING

Our land is shrinking
Down to the size of a molecule
And our growth is stunted

We walk into our homes
Speaking to our small ones in our Spirit's tongue
But … they call back to us in a strange voice

DOES ANYONE HEAR?

We want to share
To others the beauty gathered over centuries
Which we must preserve

It was given to us
By the Great Spirit who gave us this land
Now … it is here for universal sharing

WE WILL SHOUT FOR JOY!

Native Son

They have taken you from your home
Stolen the land where you once freely roamed
Tried to tell you that you had to improve
But the only one who heard was the Spirit

You must be freed from
They war that they plan
Let the Great Spirit
Cover the land

Native Son,
They have captured your will
Taken all the treasures that you made from dust
Turned all your symbols of protection and peace
Into weapons of destruction in their world of disease

You must be freed from
The war that they plan
Let the Great Spirit
Watch over the land

Native Son,
They have shrunken your deeds
To take away for all their self-serving needs
They never realized that the earth where we walk
Was not created for their hunters to stalk

You must be freed from
The damage they do
Let the Spirit bring back
The land that belongs to you

Native Son, Native Son, Teach us,
Native Son

Essays

Essays

By David H. Hill

The last year of my life has taught me that life is not a long boring experience, but rather it is a short exciting generation of wonderful opportunities for growth and being. Life is given to us because we have many messages to offer and lessons to learn. In short, life is a gift. Let us discover continuously what it has to offer us.

Life as a whole is not fair. That is correct, yes. Our remedy to life's unfairness is to find a pot of gold at the end of the rainbow, find the sunshine on the cloudy day, and start to believe that there are times when life IS fair. When I suffered a stroke five years ago, I was very angry until I realized that I am merely faced with something to overcome and I am going to come out of this smiling. Yes, for a year or two, life was not fair, but as I looked in my daughter's eyes while she said, "You can do it!" I learned that if life is not quite fair, just smile and you will see that it is fair!

Words do not necessarily have to be spoken, although they can be, to offer strength. I remember a beautiful memory from a time early in my treatment for a stroke. I was brought into the therapy room and there in front of me was a poster on the wall depicting an awesome mountain. The words printed were, "It matters not if you are the biggest, the best, or the fastest. What really matters is that you try." From that point on, it has made all the difference in the world to me. No matter what happens to me, I have the strength to try and I WILL be ever thankful to God for giving me that strength.

These essays are excerpts which were written in 2000 by David Hill for the *Essex County Hospital Observer* when he was a patient at the hospital.

If we truly examine what we have instead of what we want, we will most certainly realize that we are very rich indeed. We are blessed with intelligence, compassion, patience, modesty and humility. All of these qualities which many of us possess are worth far more than anything we might want or desire. These are all wonderful qualities which many of us could benefit from certainly if we are wise enough to share them with others.

Happiness been the most important choice I believe I have ever made in my life. Sadly, it has taken most of my life and a trip to this hospital to realize that I could be happy. Since my decision to be happy, I have found that the things that once made me angry and upset are not part of me and that which makes me happy is mine to love and share throughout eternity. I strongly believe that everyone has the choice to be happy, once they realize that happiness lives inside of them.

As we go through life, we discover what is good and positive about ourselves – and at some point, after our teen-age years, we begin to see these good qualities in others who we find and can befriend. As these qualities improve in ourselves and our self-appreciation increases, so grows our fondness for those who are like us in having that which is good and positive. It is a wonderful realization when we notice our friends imitate what we like about ourselves. So go ahead and be as good a "you" as you can, because you just might see your reflection in someone else someday.

Many of us learn best by watching the actions of those we care about and respect. We might not be convinced that an action is correct until someone we favor does it. It then becomes more meaningful when they have done it and it becomes part of us.

It is very helpful to any and all of us to be grateful when our fortune is good, because human nature causes us to be pleased in such a situation. It is difficult, however, to exhibit grace when our mood is not good. Wisdom does tell us that when we feel bad, we need to allow the discomfort to pass and still remain patient and graceful until it is no longer ours.

Being thankful is definitely a way to bring joy into your life. I have found a very personal way of being thankful and have been rewarded greatly for it. Not long after I was admitted here, I began meditating as a way of focusing on the mor positive things in life. I must say that all meditation must have a purpose and it is hoped that the purpose is somehow an act of kindness. Early in September, I began to focus my meditations on being thankful for something to enjoy. Since I began meditating in this way, I have been much happier and more receptive to change. I suggest to you then to find something to be thankful for each day, and to express that pleasant feeling as often as you can.

One's attitude is very often what people see in us and thereby form opinions which depend to a great deal on how positive or negative our attitude is. If we present a positive, happy attitude, people will see us as cheerful and want to be around us. If we present a negative, mean attitude, others will be repelled away from us. It is wise to remember our attitudes are formed inside of us, in that "the outer reflects the inner." That is, if people like us, they will copy any of our behavior that lifts them up.

Happiness is indeed a choice because in order to be truly happy, a person does not need a great deal of money or belongings. Becoming happy occurs when we strive to accept ourselves and everything around us. Once we accept the world for what it is, we become part of a world that is pleasant to us and we wish to become more like those around us. It is also possible that when others see that we have changed and become like them, they may wish to become more like us and the goodness within them is multiplied. To put it briefly, once we see goodness, we become goodness.

There is more in life than to learn as I patiently live each day I must forever strive to unlearn. For to unlearn is to see the light. It is not only wise to know what to do, it is truly wise to know what not to do.

By looking inside myself, I understand what is truly me and what has no place in who I am. In all my mystery, I fully hope to bring much life to others because when I look inside myself, I know that I am true and good. I hope that within my life there are others that I can fulfill.

- - - - - - - - - -

Over two years ago, I came to this hospital with a suicidal depression, not knowing if I wanted to live or why I would live if I did. I found the answer just over a year after coming here; God is the answer. God will love us no matter what we do. He loves us so much that He sent His son, Jesus, to die on a cross for our sins. God is the best friend you will ever have and He is there if you are lonely or confused. Inside the Bible we can find great comfort in John 14:1-18 which tells us that if we are troubled, wherever we are, God will be with us, loving us. I am very thankful that God has given me happiness with the joy of loving Him.

It is part of our lives to wonder why we are living. This question is very difficult to answer in human terms, but it can be answered in spiritual terms, by saying God loves me, or by saying God makes me happy to be alive. It does take time to be happy, but this is truly what God wants for us. He wants us to be happy and He is never going to rush us in our efforts to be happy. God loves to help us. This love is why we can understand that we are spiritual beings who are alive only to understand God's love for us and learn that His love will always be there for every one of us. Praise God for giving us the possibility of loving Him in all that we do.

The way to deal with fear is to offer it to God. God sees way beyond even our most important fears and offers us His light to guide us through our lives. God also teaches us to love what is good and hate what is bad. This gives us the choice not only to see the miraculous as possible but by God's grace to look forward to meeting it.

By living only for today, we are likely to lose sight of the truly amazing gift that God has for us when our life on earth is over. That gift is Heaven. The grace of God which offers this gift to us urges us to live not only for today or tomorrow, but for eternity. God's love is another gift which God will never stop giving to us. We can offer Him acknowledgement by offering love, kindness and caring to those around us; where we live; where we work; everywhere we go. God's love will always continue to grow. Our thanks to Him is to offer it to others.

Until recently, birthdays for me have been periods where I just wished I were younger than I am. Something has happened this year that has changed my view: I have looked at my belief in God and found that by looking at Him as a permanent improvement to my life who can change me for the better in all I do. I started loving myself more because His love is always there. I will turn forty-seven, **Praise God**, in August, and I live myself much more than last year as I turned forty-six. I thank God for that and look forward to loving Him more as I learn of the endless beauty of His love as my life unfolds.

- - - - - - - - - -

Hobbies can enrich your life by providing ways for you to develop your interests. It is true that many people enjoy reading. Reading provides a way to learn more about what interests you. This learning will make you happy by giving you more to think about and will offer you chances to discuss what you have read. Other hobbies will have a similar effect, such as running, walking, hiking, and swimming. Whatever hobby you choose, choose one you like and do it as often as you can.

- - - - - - - - - -

There was a wonderful carnival on Wednesday, September 13, 2000, in the evening. There was a ball toss game and many nice gifts and clothes to buy. There was a wonderful dinner with hot dogs, chicken, hamburgers, potato salad and chips, and of course soda. The recreation staff did a wonderful job of serving delicious food and very bright smiles. It was really great fun. There was also music and dancing.

- - - - - - - - - -

The month of December started off with some very beautiful music selections sung by the Performance Group on Thursday the seventh. There was a very large audience who sang along very happily to "Jingle Bell Rock" and "Frosty the Snowman," and in a great way made this evening a very happy one. As a member of the Performance Group, I want to say it was a great pleasure singing for such a pleasant audience. It was a wonderful evening and a great joy singing early in December and I will remember this concert for a long time.

- - - - - - - - - -

Xenophon once said "the sweetest of all sounds is praise." This is certainly true because I have received praise on days when I have not even wanted to get out of bed. These words gave me a sense that beautiful music had come to my ears. I truly hope that you have had the joy of receiving such a compliment because it really can make your day.

- - - - - - - - - -

Peace is a wonderful quality that takes great thought and real effort to achieve. It can only develop inside you and cannot be truly found in another's habits even if those habits seem peaceful.

Real peace begins with accepting the things about us that we would rather not have and forgiving ourselves for having these qualities. Once they are accepted, we can refuse to accept the negative effect they have had on us. If we continue this acceptance of everything good or bad inside us, we will learn that there is peace inside us in the empty space where the negative qualities once stood. If you let this peace continue to grow, the greater it gets, the more visible it will be to others, and hopefully they will want it, too.

Grace is the inward solitude ability to accept or tolerate that which we might not be happy with, and to do so in as pleasant a manner as possible. When we begin to use grace to accept such things, we have then expressed to God that we are open and accepting of His love and His healing. There are some things in our lives that can be changed. It is wise to become aware that those things which can be changed, will be changed with God's help, if we ask Him. He is always there to help us. God has created each of us knowing that we will change and promising to help us change. It is also true that He will help us to know why a change occurs when it happens or not long thereafter.

What is love? The most special, comforting and fulfilling love is the love that God has given to people ever since He made Adam and Eve in the Garden of Eden. Adam and Eve were made so they could share God's love with each other. I believe there is a similar reason that God made us: He had so much love that He wanted to give it to others forever. This love or devotion is so real that only God could have created it. This is what love is. In short, God's love is given to us because He loves us and wants us to give this love to Him by giving it to others, also.

- - - - - - - - - -

Acknowledgements

Miss Floreen Henry

There is a very nice attendant on the 7-3 shift on Ward 35 named Miss Floreen Henry. She is very pleasant to be around as well as being great at finding art projects for those on the ward. She is always in a very pleasant mood and is a joy to be around. We are lucky to have Miss Henry with us on 35 and we hope she will be here for a long time. Thank you for being yourself and being so thoughtful.

Mabel Davis, Recreation Therapy Aide

Mabel is on the Recreation Therapy staff. Mabel supervises the free recreation periods in the evenings and also manages the library in the Vocational Rehabilitation wing of the Activity Building Tuesday through Thursday afternoons from 1:00 p.m. to 2:30 p.m. She has a very pleasant disposition and seems to really love being here and helping us. Thank you so much, Mabel, for bringing your joy to evening free time and God bless you for being here.

Connie Mooney, Music Therapist

It becomes instantly clear as soon as I enter Connie's room and see her that she is in love with music. I would like to thank Connie for the many very enjoyable music groups I have had with her. When I came to this hospital almost two years ago, I had a few negative feelings in general about music, which Connie has turned into joyous feelings with her overflowing knowledge of and joy for music. Connie was born to bring joyful music to people and we are all blessed that she is here to brighten our days. Connie, you are truly one of a kind. Thank you so much for offering me so much pleasant music over the last two years. You are extraordinary!

- - - - - - - - - -

I gratefully open my heart to the following very special people —

George J. Hill: My extremely compassionate stepfather, who always reminded me in my deepest pain that I was going to be able to walk about again if I just believed that I could.

Helene Z. Hill: My loving mother who constantly acknowledged my pain and fear and reminded me that if I continued to believe that my weakness would continue to exist, it would. It is with her help that I have continued to heal even in times of insurmountable doubt and apprehension.

James W. Hill: My extremely caring and fair-minded brother who helped me to always believe that each of us must be loved and treated fairly with no prejudgment of any sort. It was Jim's concern (particularly on Christmas of 1995 when he welcomed me into his home to spend the holiday) that convinced me that I was special and certainly no less loveable because of my stroke.

Sarah Hill: My eldest sister, who has traveled widely in Europe and Central America, bringing with her a constantly growing and nourishing love and compassion for all people, which surpassed any disadvantages that they might be forced to contend with. She brought back to me a special love for my pain and various avocations and nurtured my interests so that my mind would continually focus on what I could do rather than what I was no longer able to do.

Helena R. Hill (Lana): My youngest sister, who for many years has been teaching rock climbing and survival skills through much of the Eastern U.S. She has developed and nurtured her own special breed of love and concern. She has, in my pain and agony, constantly encouraged me to love myself as much as possible and in so doing gave me much more room in my heart to love and care for others.

Sheri: My loving wife from 1981 to 1983. Sheri, I cannot find words to explain how grateful I am that you stayed beside me during our marriage in the early nineteen eighties. I am immeasurably grateful for your present in my life then, because it made the stroke that I suffered one decade later simply a matter of following the phoenix and rising from the flames of my injury. You gave me your friendship then when I was at my loneliest without you, and that friendship is still resting in my heart and will be there for you if you ever need it. It is because of your great compassion that Heather is as understanding and loving as she is.

Heather: My brilliant adolescent daughter who has always stood by me and loved me through the darkest, most difficult seasons following my stroke. Heather showered me with gifts in Thanksgiving of 1994, the sentimental value of which far outvalued their usefulness and reminded me that her love would always be there for me. Heather, my love is always there for you, now and in Heaven when we meet after we pass from this earth.

Henry Keuchenmeister: I will talk about Henry last, but surely not least, because he was a caring friend all through my High School years in St. Louis, Missouri. Henry was a friend and ally to me.

Index of Titles, First Lines, and Sections

Titles are in *italics*. Titles shown in [*brackets*] were originally untitled.
Sections are in **bold.**

ANNOTATED BIBLIOGRAPHY

[*Holy Bible*] *The Layman's Parallel Bible*. Grand Rapids, Mich.: The Zondervan Corporation, 1973. Contains four parallel translations: King James Version [KJV], Modern Language Bible, Living Bible, and Revised Standard Version [RSV].

The Book of Common Prayer and Administration of the Sacraments and Other Rites and Ceremonies of the Church: According to the use of The Episcopal Church. New York: The Seabury Press, 1979.

The Hymnal of the Protestant Episcopal Church in the United States of America. New York: The Church Pension Fund, 1940.

The Book of Mormon, Another Testament of Jesus Christ. Salt Lake City, Utah: The Church of Jesus Christ of Latter-day Saints, 2009. Based on Joseph Smith, Jr., *The Book of Mormon: An Account Written by the Hand of Mormon, Upon Plates Taken from the Plates of Nephi.* Palmyra, N.Y.: E. B. Grandin, Publisher, 1830.

Encyclopædia Britannica. Encyclopædia Britannica Deluxe Edition. Chicago: Encyclopædia Britannica, 2013. References to Buddhism, including hypertext references to aspects of Buddhism that appear in David Hill's poetry and essays: bodhisattva, Eightfold Path, enlightenment, Four Noble Truths, Jains, Karma, Nirvana, reality, Theravada ("Way of the Elders"), Triratna, Upanishads, vedana, Vedas, Vishnu, and Zen; Hare Krishna, including Bhagavadgita; Rastafari (Rastafarianism); Autism and autism spectrum disorders (ASD); and Epilepsy, including grand mal and petit mal.

Cobbs, Marnie. Poetry. "Diminishment," for my father during his depression, https://www.nh.gov/nharts/artsandartists/poetshowcase2/poetlaureate12.html (accessed August 30, 2021).

_____. *Swimming Poems*. Eaton, N.H.: The Uphill House, 1998.

Internet sources:

Temporal Lobe Epilepsy: https://www.epilepsy.com/learn/types-epilepsy-syndromes/temporal-lobe-epilepsy-aka-tle (accessed August 30, 2021).

Congenital analgesia (Congenital Insensitivity to Pain; CIP): https://medlineplus.gov/genetics/condition/congenital-insensitivity-to-pain/ (accessed August 30, 2021).

Hall, Donald, Robert Pack, and Louis Simpson. *The New Poets of England and America.* New York: Meridian Books, 1957. Includes Robert Layzer by name in the list of poets selected. It was published in the year that Layzer graduated from medical school.

Hill, Essie Mae. *Prairie Daughter: Stories and Poems from Iowa.* Berwyn Heights, Md.: Heritage Books, 2019. David Hill studied his grandmother's poems in this book

Hill, George J. *Western Pilgrims: The Hill, Stockwell and Allied Families. Ancestors and Descendants of George J. Hill and Jessie Fidelia Stockwell, Who Were Married in Wright County, Iowa, in 1882.* Berwyn Heights, Md.: Heritage Books, 2014. David Hill's immediate family and his step-cousins are in this book.

_____. *Quakers and Pilgrims: The Shoemaker, Warren and Allied Families. Ancestors and Descendants of William Toy Shoemaker and Mabel Warren, Who Were Married in Philadelphia in 1895.* Berwyn Heights, Md.: Heritage Books, 2015. David Hill's mother's family and his cousins in her family are in this book.

Lawler, Kara, and Regan Long. *A Letter for Every Mother.* New York: Center Street, 2018.

Lawler, Kara. *Everywhere Holy: Seeing Beauty, Remembering Your Identity, and Finding God Right Where You Are*. Nashville, Tenn.: Nelson Books, 2019.

Lippman, Alan. Medical History Society of New Jersey / Publications / Book Reviews. https://www.mhsnj.org/book-reviews (accessed August 31, 2021)

Oliver, Mary. *Devotions.* New York: Penguin RandomHouse LLC, [2017] 2020.

Rubenstein, Howard, and Max Lee. *Romance of the Western Chamber—a Musical* (La Jolla, Calif.: Granite Hills Press, 2012). Howard Rubenstein and his wife Judith worked as a team on this and many other books and musical productions.

Rubenstein, Judith S. *The Christmas Present.* San Diego, Calif.: Granite Hills Press, [1994] 2019.

_____. *Preparing a Child for a Good-bye Visit to a Dying Loved One. JAMA* 247 (no. 18, 27 May1982): 2571-2.

Tolkien, J. R. *The Hobbit. Lord of the Rings.*
Tolkien's life story, his interests, and his imagination of fantasy played an important role in David Hill's thoughts. For example, see "The Maker and the Poet" and "Silence" in *A Lesson in Reality.*

ABOUT THE AUTHOR

David **Hedgcock Hill**, 48, a poet and musician who resided at Ivy Hill, Newark, New Jersey, died at Mountainside Hospital, Montclair, on January 4, 2004, of complications from a stroke on November 25, 2003. Mr. Hill was born in Boston, Massachusetts, on August 29, 1955, the son of James Hedgcock Grover, Esq., and his wife, the former Helene Zimmermann of Haverford, Pennsylvania. In 1964 he was adopted by his stepfather and his surname was legally changed to Hill.

As a child, Mr. Hill was a student at the Park School, Brookline, Massachusetts, and in 1975 he graduated from University City (Missouri) High School. He later attended Fontbonne College, Clayton, Missouri, and Glenville (West Virginia) State College. In 1981 he married a college classmate, Sheri Lynn Wilson, with whom he had one child, a daughter. They were divorced in 1983 and his former wife died in February 2003.

Mr. Hill was employed for several years as a Nursing Assistant at Saint Barnabas Medical Center, Livingston, New Jersey. In 1994 he became completely disabled as the result of an accident in which his carotid artery was damaged, producing a massive stroke with paralysis of his left arm. Prior to his stroke, Mr. Hill had composed and played music for the piano and organ, and he had written and published poetry. Following his stroke, he continued to play the piano with his right hand and write essays and poetry, principally on themes of spirituality, love, and loneliness.

Mr. Hill is survived by his parents, Helene Zimmermann Hill, Ph.D., and George J. Hill, M.D., of West Orange, New Jersey, and Eaton, New Hampshire; and by his biological father, James Grover, of Ashland, New Hampshire; a brother, James Hill, of Poughkeepsie, New York; three half-sisters, Sarah Hill of Kalamazoo, Michigan, Helena Hill of Baltimore, Maryland, and Robin Grover of Concord, New Hampshire; and a daughter, Mrs. Heather Dawn Hill Haught, of Parkersburg, West Virginia.

A memorial service will be held at the Church of the Holy Innocents, 681 Prospect Avenue, West Orange, New Jersey, at 11:00 a.m., on Saturday, January 10, and his cremains will be interred at Parkersburg, West Virginia.

Donations in his memory may be made to the Brain Injury Association of New Jersey, Inc., 1090 King George Post Road, Suite 708, Edison, NJ 08837. [*]

HILL - David Hedgcock, of Newark, on Sunday, Jan. 4, 2004, beloved father of Heather Dawn Hill Haught of Parkersburg, W. Va., loving son of Helene Zimmermann Hill, Ph.D. and George J. Hill, M.D. of West Orange and Eaton, N.H., and his biological father, James Grover of Ashland, N.H., loving brother of James Hill of Poughkeepsie, N.Y., and loving half brother to three sisters, Sarah Hill of Kalamazoo, Mich., Helena Hill of Baltimore, Md., and Robin Grover of Concord, N.H. A memorial service will be held at the Church of the Holy Innocents, 681 Prospect Ave., West Orange, N.J., at 11 a.m. on Saturday, Jan. 10, and his cremains will be interred at Parkersburg, W.Va. Arrangements are by The DANGLER FUNERAL HOME OF WEST ORANGE, 340 Main St., West Orange, N.J. (973-325-1212). Donations in his memory may be made to the Brain Injury Association of New Jersey Inc., 1090 King George Post Rd., Suite 708, Edison, N.J. 08837. Communications may be sent to the Hill Family at ghill@ drew.edu. [†]

David Hedgcock Hill is shown in the Church of the Holy Innocents Burial List in West Orange, N.J. In addition to the burial of his cremains in Parkersburg, W. Va., beside his wife, some of his ashes were interred in the memorial garden adjacent to the church, with his name inscribed on a stone. Other ashes of his were buried in the Hill Family Plot in the Snowville Cemetery, Eaton, New Hampshire. [‡]

[*] Obituary composed for the Program of David Hill's Memorial Service.
[†] Newark (NJ) *Star-Ledger* (6-7 January 2004)   Obituaries
https://obits.nj.com/us/obituaries/starledger/name/david-hill-obituary?pid=1771409 (accessed August 23, 2021)
[‡] https://peoplelegacy.com/cemetery/holy_innocents_cemetery-2m1k01/ (accessed August 23, 2021)

Editor's Note:

Not mentioned in the Obituary and Notices are several other important aspects of David Hill's life.

Throughout his childhood, from earliest days until he was in his late 'teens, he suffered from an affliction that defied diagnosis and treatment. He would have sudden periods of unconsciousness, which were troubling to watch and which often placed him in great danger. Were these seizures a form of epilepsy, or were they a manifestation of a metabolic disorder? Were they psychosomatic – a cry for attention – or were they an unusual form of autism? The seizures, which his family called "spells," were studied by the most famous neurologists in Boston and at the National Institutes of Health. The "spells" sometimes seemed to respond to drinking of sugary liquids. All of the possibilities were considered, from temporal lobe epilepsy to abnormal bursts of pancreatic secretion of insulin. Strangely, David's "spells" gradually became less frequent. He was able to move from special schools to attend public high school as a senior. It was a proud and happy day for David and his family when he marched in the Commencement procession.

He gradually developed the ability to go on long walks alone. He was able to ride a bicycle for great distances, sometimes staying overnight far out in the country with minimal cover. Before he had his stroke, he successfully completed a course to become a Nursing Assistant. His hospital work included the use of great physical strength, which he developed as a result of his long walks and bicycle riding. He enjoyed hiking with his family on vacation in New Hampshire. One of the memorable experiences we had of David was to see him riding happily on a small orange tractor, mowing a field near our farm house. He then rode on the tractor's platform behind a young Hungarian boy who was staying with us for the summer. He taught our visitor how to start the tractor, shift the gears, and mow.

David also had difficulty sensing pain. This is a condition known as congenital analgesia. Although his congenital insensitivity to pain (CIP), as it is called, was incomplete, it was manifested in many ways. He would have a laceration of the skin or fracture a bone, without recognizing that it had happened until someone else noticed it and he then sought treatment. By the time he went to college, he was clearly aware of the problem, and would be careful to watch for injuries that needed medical attention.

David's search for Truth began while he was in college, and it never ended. He was baptized and confirmed as an Episcopalian, and he served as a young acolyte in the church. He underwent full-immersion adult baptism when he married a woman who was a Baptist. After they were divorced, he underwent the ceremony again to become a member of the Church of Jesus Christ of Latter Day Saints. At the same time, he continued to play the organ and worship with his parents in the Episcopal Church, observing the rite of Holy Communion. David studied other religions, too. His search for Truth and the Way included the study of Zen Buddhism and Hare Krishna, and – because of his musical interest in reggae – Rastafarianism. These belief systems influenced his poetry, the lyrics for his music, and his essays. However, he rarely quoted Biblical scripture or any of the sacred writings of other faiths. He was familiar with Book of Mormon and the King James Version because of his study of religious texts with Mormons and Baptists. However, he favored modern translations of the Bible into simple English. After reaching a plateau in recovery from his stroke, he gradually developed serenity and peace of mind that was very affecting to others. He became a lay minister to those in need.

About the Editor

(c) JanPressPhotomedia, Livingston, NJ

George J. Hill is a fifth-generation Iowan. He graduated from high school in Sac City, Iowa, and then attended Yale University, where he majored in history. He graduated from Harvard Medical School, and after forty years as a practicing surgeon, he is now Emeritus Professor of Surgery at Rutgers-New Jersey Medical School. He served in the U.S. Marine Corps and the U.S. Public Health Service, and he was awarded the Meritorious Service Medal upon retirement as a Captain, Medical Corps, in the U.S. Navy. Dr. Hill also earned an M.A. in history at Rutgers University and a D.Litt. in history from Drew University. He has written or edited more than 20 books on medicine and surgery, family history and genealogy, environmental history and international relations.

Other Books by the Editor

Medicine and Science

Leprosy in Five Young Men
Outpatient Surgery (3 editions; 2 translated into Spanish as *Cirugia Menor*)
Clinical Oncology, with John Horton

History

Edison's Environment (3 editions)
Intimate Relationships: The U.S. and Liberia, 1917-1947 (3 editions)
Proceed to Peshawar

Heritage Books by George J. Hill:

A Lesson in Reality: Poems and Essays
By David Hedgcock Hill
Edited by George J. Hill, M.D.

*American Dreams: Ancestors and Descendants of John Zimmermann and
Eva Katherine Kellenbenz, Who Were Married in Philadelphia in 1885*

*"Dearest Barb": From Karachi, 1943–1945, Letters and Photographs
in the World War II Papers of a Naval Intelligence Officer,
Lieutenant Albert Zimmermann, USNR*

Edison's Environment: The Great Inventor Was Also a Great Polluter

Four Families: A Tetralogy Reader's Guide to Western Pilgrims, Quakers
and Puritans, Fundy to Chesapeake, *and* American Dreams;
*Synopsis of 481 Immigrants and First Known Ancestors
in America from Northern Europe in the Families of
George J. Hill and Jessie F. Stockwell,
William T. Shoemaker and Mabel Warren,
William H. Thompson and Sarah D. Rundall,
John Zimmermann and Eva K. Kellenbenz,
with Outlines of Their Descent from the Immigrants*

*Fundy to Chesapeake: The Thompson, Rundall and Allied Families;
Ancestors and Descendants of William Henry Thompson and Sarah D.
Rundall, Who Were Married in Linn County, Iowa, in 1889*

Health Matters: A New View of Human History

*Hill: The Ferry Keeper's Family, Luke Hill and Mary Hout, Who Were
Married in Windsor, Connecticut, in 1651 and Fourteen Generations
of Their Known and Possible Descendants*

John Saxe, Loyalist (1732–1808) and His Descendants for Five Generations

Prairie Daughter: Stories and Poems from Iowa by Essie Mae Thompson Hill

*Quakers and Puritans: The Shoemaker, Warren and Allied Families;
Ancestors and Descendants of William Toy Shoemaker and Mabel Warren,
Who Were Married in Philadelphia in 1895*

*Rolling with Patton: The Letters and Photographs of Field Director Gerald
L. Hill, 303rd Infantry Regiment, 97th "Trident" Division, 1943–1945*

*The Home Front in World War II: From the Letters of
Essie Mae Hill to Field Director Gerald L. Hill*

*War Letters, 1917–1918: From Dr. William T. Shoemaker, A.E.F.,
in France, and His Family in Philadelphia*

Three Men in a Jeep Called "Ma Kabul," Script for a Movie:
A True Story of High Adventure by Three Allied
Intelligence Officers in World War II

Western Pilgrims: The Hill, Stockwell and Allied Families;
Ancestors and Descendants of George J. Hill and
Jessie Fidelia Stockwell, Who Were Married
in Wright County, Iowa, in 1882

www.ingramcontent.com/pod-product-compliance
Lightning Source LLC
Chambersburg PA
CBHW071101090426
42737CB00013B/2412